Pam Cat

Written by Catherine Baker

Illustrated by Fran and David Brylewski

Collins

It is not mud.

It is Pam Cat.

Pam is in muck.

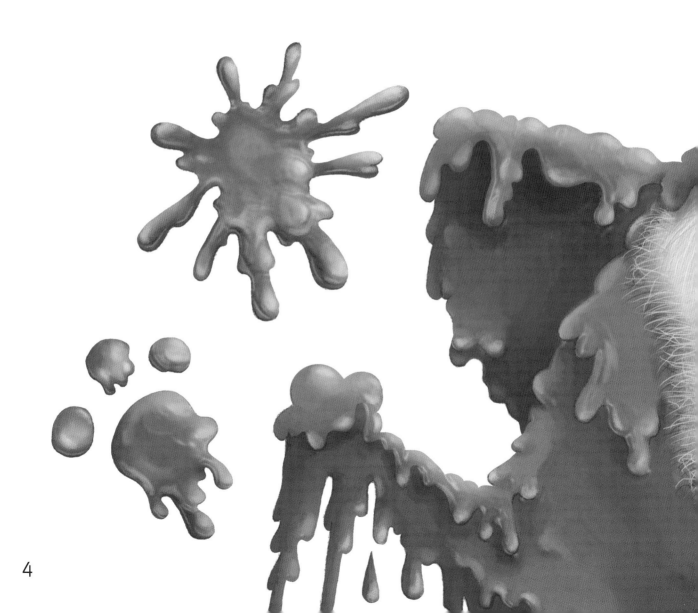

Pam Cat is sad.

It is Tim Dog.

Tim is a pug.

Can Tim get Pam?

No, Tim can not.

It is Kim Kid.

Can Kim get Pam?

Kim is in the muck.

Kim can get Pam Cat!

🐾 After reading 🐾

Letters and Sounds: Phase 2

Word count: 50

Focus phonemes: /g/ /o/ /c/ /k/ /e/ /u/ ck

Common exception words: is, no, the

Curriculum links: Understanding the World: The World

Early learning goals: Understanding: answer "how" and "why" questions in response to stories; Reading: read and understand simple sentences, read some common irregular words

Developing fluency

- Your child may enjoy hearing you read the book.
- Look at page 8. Point to the question mark. Ask your child if they know what it is. Now model reading the question with the appropriate intonation.
- Ask your child to read the question on page 11.

Phonic practice

- Look at the word **muck** on page 4. Model sound talking and blending the word, m/u/ck, **muck**. Point out that "ck" usually comes at the end of, or near the end of, a word.
- Try writing out a few more words that end with "ck". (e.g. *chick, pick, pack*) Ask your child to sound talk and blend them. Can they think of any others?
- Look at the "I spy sounds" pages (14–15). Say the sounds together. How many items can your child spot that have the /u/ sound in them (e.g. *pug, mug, umbrella, cup, cupcake, duck*) or "ck" in them? (e.g. *chick, duck, truck*)

Extending vocabulary

- Ask your child to find the odd one out in each of the following sets of synonyms (you may wish to read the words to your child).

mud	muck	ice	(*ice*)
excited	sad	unhappy	(*excited*)
jump	sit	leap	(*sit*)
help	ignore	support	(*ignore*)